THE OFFICIAL
QUEENS PARK RANGERS
ANNUAL 2026

Written by Francis Atkinson and Matt Webb
Designed by Daniel Brawn

A Grange Publication

© 2025. Published by Grange Communications Ltd., Edinburgh, under licence from Queens Park Rangers. Grange Communications Ltd., 25 Herbert Place, Dublin, D02 AY86. frontdesk@grangecommunications.co.uk Printed in Romania.

Every effort has been made to ensure the accuracy of information within this publication but the publishers cannot be held responsible for any errors or omissions. Views expressed are those of the author and do not necessarily represent those of the publishers or the football club. All rights reserved.

Photographs © Rex Features.

ISBN 978-1-917538-47-3

CONTENTS

06 FRESH THREADS
QPR's 2025/26 home strip reviewed

08 JULIEN JOINS
Welcoming new QPR head coach, Julien Stéphan

13 GOT, GOT, NEED!
Our Sky Bet Championship opponents

14 THE ALTERNATIVES
Looking at our away and third strips for '25/26

16 THE NEWBIES
A look at our summer signings

24 JOB DUNNE
Jimmy's 2024/25 awards sweep

26 FOCUS ON
Nicolas Madsen in the spotlight

28 YOU ARE THE REF
Take up the whistle in our annual favourite

34 THE STORY OF 1975/76
Reviewing our best-ever season, 50 years on

38 ALL THE GOALS
The pick from 2024/25

42 FOCUS ON
Harvey Vale in the spotlight

44 GAMES & FUN
Solve our R's-themed trivia

48 FOCUS ON
Michi Frey in the spotlight

50 QUIZ
How well do you remember last season?

56 FOCUS ON
Kieran Morgan in the spotlight

61 QUIZ AND PUZZLE ANSWERS

62 FIXTURES
Our 2025/26 schedule

CELEBRATING 1975/76
WITH OUR NEW HOME KIT

OUR home kit for the 2025/26 campaign is a tribute to the iconic QPR side of 1975/76, 50 years on!

That unforgettable season saw Rangers finish second by a single point in the First Division and qualify for Europe. Half a century later, our traditional blue and white hoops proudly honour the team's achievement and lasting legacy.

This season's design features a subtle chequered pattern woven into the blue hoops, inspired by the matchday programme covers from that era. Continuing the theme seen in our away and third kits, the classic stick man illustration - prominent in our programmes throughout the seventies - appears on the back of the collar.

Inside the neck tape, the message reads: THEN. NOW. FOREVER. QPR - a constant theme across all our new kits.

The shirt features blue detailing throughout, with sponsor logos in white positioned within the blue hoops.

To mark the launch, the campaign brought together QPR legends Phil Parkes and Gerry Francis from the 1975/76 side alongside current players from both the men's and women's teams - connecting our rich past with those shaping the club's future.

Completing the kit, the white shorts feature a blue cuff with the smart chequered design, while the socks are predominantly white with blue detailing.

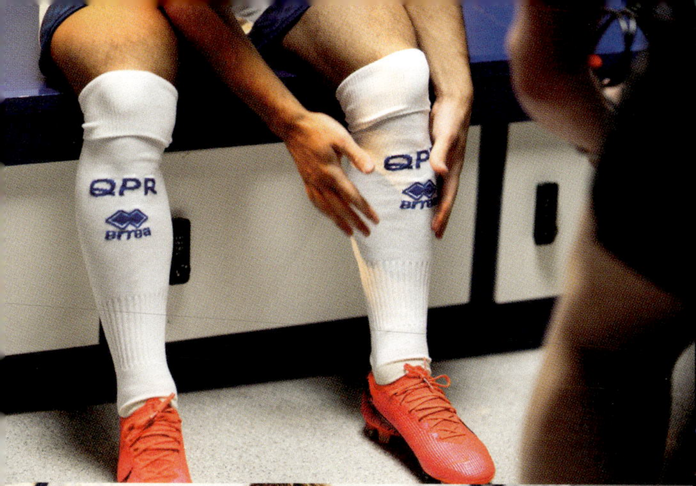

SUPPORTERS CAN NOW PURCHASE THE NEW HOME SHIRT ONLINE OR IN PERSON AT THE STADIUM SUPERSTORE, ALONGSIDE OUR FULL 2025/26 RANGE.

BIENVENUE, JULIEN!

QPR were delighted to confirm Julien Stéphan as the club's new head coach in late June.

The 44-year-old has previously worked in the French top flight with Rennes and Strasbourg.

He guided his boyhood club Rennes to their first trophy in 48 years when they won the Coupe de France in 2019, and achieved their highest league placement in their history in 2019/20 when they finished third in Ligue 1 to qualify for the Champions League.

Under the Frenchman, Strasbourg finished sixth in the table in 2021/22, recording their highest position for 42 years.

Now Stéphan is ready for a new chapter in W12.

"I feel very proud and excited to join QPR," he said.

"QPR is a historic club with strong values and passionate fans, so I feel honoured.

"I wanted to come here because I know there's a lot of passion around the club and around the team, and I feel very lucky to discover that.

"There is something unique about English football. The intensity, the atmosphere, the passion of the fans also, the tempo of the game, the culture around the club all make it a very stimulating environment for a coach."

Explaining how he likes to play the game, Stéphan said: "I like my team to play with intensity, energy and personality.

"THE MAIN VALUES ARE COMMITMENT, DISCIPLINE, AND TEAM SPIRIT"

"I believe in collective organisation and also clear identity - but also in giving players freedom to express themselves. I like courage and I want brave players – they are the players who take initiative because I think to have emotion in football, we have to take risks."

While keen to bring energy and excitement to W12, Stéphan said there are fundamentals he demands from all his players.

"The main values are commitment, discipline, and team spirit," he said.

"I expect my players to give everything on the pitch for the team, for the fans, and to show the right attitude.

"The shirt deserves respect, total respect, and it's non-negotiable for me."

Stéphan has built a reputation for player development on the Continent, and he revealed his philosophy to maximise the potential of who he coaches. "For me, each player is different," he explained. "Most important is to understand their personality, their strengths and also what motivates them.

"I try to build a strong relationship with them and create the conditions to put them in the right environment to develop."

Looking ahead to life as QPR's head coach, Stéphan said: "I see a group with talent, commitment and potential. I think for sure there's work to do, but I think we have great potential in the squad and there's a strong foundation to develop."

Stéphan is excited to have the QPR fans with him, adding: "Their support will be essential.

"We need them. We need to fight for them and I hope they feel proud of what they see on the pitch. We need them in the good moments and also in the tough ones.

"We are ready to give our best and to start this new chapter with determination and ambition."

CEO Christian Nourry said: "It is with great pleasure that we welcome Julien and appoint him as head coach.

"Julien's track record of developing young players into world class talent was a major factor in our decision to appoint him. Alongside this, both at Rennes and Strasbourg, he achieved historic league success.

"He has demonstrated genuine excitement about our players in the first-team squad and the prospect of working with them to try to push this club on further.

"Julien's appointment is the fruit of an extensive process that was undertaken by key club figures to identify, evaluate and recruit a coach that understands the club's football philosophy and is energised by it."

GOT, GOT, NEED!

Here's a map containing all of QPR's 2025/26 Sky Bet Championship opponents.

These include Ipswich Town, Leicester City and Southampton – all relegated from the Premier League last season.

Also competing at this level for '25/26 are Birmingham City, Wrexham and Charlton Athletic following their respective promotions from League One.

How many new grounds will you be visiting this season? Tick them off as you go and jot down how many games you attended at the end of the campaign!

- [ ] 1. Birmingham City
- [ ] 2. Blackburn Rovers
- [ ] 3. Bristol City
- [ ] 4. Charlton Athletic
- [ ] 5. Coventry City
- [ ] 6. Derby County
- [ ] 7. Hull City
- [ ] 8. Ipswich Town
- [ ] 9. Leicester City
- [ ] 10. Middlesbrough
- [ ] 11. Millwall
- [ ] 12. Norwich City
- [ ] 13. Oxford United
- [ ] 14. Portsmouth
- [ ] 15. Preston North End
- [ ] 16. Sheffield United
- [ ] 17. Sheffield Wednesday
- [ ] 18. Southampton
- [ ] 19. Stoke City
- [ ] 20. Swansea City
- [ ] 21. Watford
- [ ] 22. West Bromwich Albion
- [ ] 23. Wrexham

TOTAL AWAY TEAMS VISITED

INTRODUCING OUR 2025/26 AWAY KIT

OUR brand-new 2025/26 away kit is a bold reimagining of a club classic.

The striking halved shirt features an eye-catching pink and black contrast, with matching detailing on the QPR and Erreà logos. The sponsors are also displayed in clean white lettering, adding to the shirt's fashionable and modern aesthetic.

Inspired by one of our most iconic away shirts - first worn 50 years ago during the memorable 1975/76 season when Rangers finished second in the First Division and ventured into Europe - the new kit pays homage to our proud history. However, the switch to pink and black gives the design a contemporary edge, appealing to both lifelong supporters and new fans alike.

Subtle touches bring extra meaning. The back of the collar features the familiar stick man illustration first seen in our early seventies matchday programmes, while the inside neck-tape reads THEN. NOW. FOREVER. QPR - a powerful reminder of our roots and our journey forward.

Comfort meets sustainability in this latest release. Made from Erreà's 'Future' fabric, the shirt not only offers top-level performance and comfort, but it's also constructed from recycled polyester, making it a more environmentally-responsible choice.

The away shirt is completed with black shorts that feature pink detailing and a matching cuff, and black socks with a bold pink band through the middle.

Also revealed are our three goalkeeper kits for the season. The home goalkeeper shirt is mainly black with sharp purple detailing. The alternate option is a stylish teal with navy accents, while the third shirt stands out in vivid orange, paired with a black collar and cuffs.

HISTORY IN THE MAKING

OUR third kit for the 2025/26 season marks the return of the much-loved green and white hoops - now updated with elegant gold detailing that also features across the sponsor logos.

It's a modern twist on a classic look that pays tribute to a significant chapter in our history - 100 years since QPR transitioned from green and white to the now-iconic blue and white hoops.

Rangers first adopted green and white in 1892, and this season marks 100 years since those colours last represented the club. Club historian Chris Guy commented: "This design marks an important milestone in celebrating our club's history. The period between 1892 and 1926, during which these colours were worn, was an important chapter in our proud heritage."

The R's entered the season in style with the return of the green and white hoops - an alternative look rooted in tradition but refreshed for the present day. A shirt that connects our rich past with our ambitions for the future.

This kit is more than just a shirt - it's a celebration of the club's history. The inside neck-tape once again features the words THEN. NOW. FOREVER. QPR. Another reminder of our history and where we're heading.

On the back of the collar, fans will recognise the familiar stick man illustration seen on our kit releases so far this season.

Crafted from Erreà's cutting-edge 'Future' fabric, the shirt delivers both performance and comfort at the highest level. It's also made from recycled polyester, reinforcing our commitment to sustainability and responsible production.

The look is completed with green shorts featuring a black cuff and gold trim, and green socks finished with a distinctive gold and black band.

THE NEWBIES

It was another busy summer transfer window in W12!
Meet our new first-team recruits for the 2025/26 Sky Bet Championship campaign...

RICHARD KONE

Richard Kone completed a permanent transfer to QPR from Wycombe Wanderers for an undisclosed fee.

The 22-year-old striker scored 21 goals in all competitions for the Chairboys last season – and was voted both EFL League One Player of the Year and Young Player of the Year in what was his first full campaign at professional level.

"It's an amazing feeling, I'm really glad to join an amazing team, a great club," Kone said. "I can't wait to get started."

Kone scored more than 120 goals in under four years at non-league level before joining Wycombe in January 2024, and his determination to make it shines through as he talks.

"I've always been really hungry to achieve being a professional footballer," he said.

"I made my mind when the opportunity comes, I'll be ready. I'll be ready to take it. By God's grace, it took the time that it took, four years, and when the time was right, I did take my chances and here I am."

After a successful 18 months at Adams Park, he is excited to continue his rise up the English football pyramid with this move to the Championship – and with many options available to him, Kone explained why a call with CEO Christian Nourry, head coach Julien Stéphan and head of recruitment Andy Belk convinced him QPR should be his next step in the professional game.

"It was a really positive chat," he said. "They showed me the project and it was really exciting."

Kone, who received his first call up for Ivory Coast U23s in May, admits he is excited to work under Stéphan, adding: "For what he has done in the past with young players, I think that as well was one of the things that pushed me.

"I want to know what it is to work under him."

Explaining his strengths as a player, and what R's fans can expect, Kone said: "I am really dynamic, like to work hard, run a lot, hold up play.

"I try my best to be better every day. I think they can expect goals from me – goals, working hard off the ball and linking up with my team-mates.

"I'll back myself and say I will score goals. I've always believed in myself, no matter the level. You still have to improve, keep on learning and add to what you have already."

AMADOU MBENGUE

Amadou Mbengue completed a permanent transfer to QPR from Reading following the expiry of his contract.

The 23-year-old comes to W12 after three seasons with the Royals, where he made 109 appearances, including 26 Championship outings during 2022/23.

Prior to his time in Berkshire, Mbengue played his football with Metz in Ligue 1 – now he is ready for his next adventure in English football.

"I am happy to be here and ready to work," said Mbengue, who had a host of Championship clubs chasing his signature.

"I was talking with Christian (Nourry, CEO) and the idea and the project he has for the club is very, very good. We are on the same page and that is why I chose QPR. They have a lot of objectives for the future."

Mbengue, who has represented Senegal at Under-23 level, has a reputation for being a big character, and he said he takes his football seriously – but makes sure he has fun, too.

"I enjoy the game and I enjoy life," he said. "After a game when we win, I'm here to enjoy it with the fans. I think it's important to make them happy.

"I'm excited to meet the fans and to take my first steps in Loftus Road."

RUMARN BURRELL

Rumarn Burrell joined QPR from Burton Albion for an undisclosed fee.

The 24-year-old striker spent 12 months with the Brewers in League One, netting 11 goals in all competitions in 2024/25.

The Jamaica international came through the ranks at Grimsby before joining Middlesbrough in 2019 at the age of 18. After loan spells with Bradford and Kilmarnock, Burrell really found his feet when he joined Falkirk three years ago, scoring 12 goals in all competitions.

A season with Cove Rangers in Scotland's third tier followed and saw Burrell net 24 goals, earning a move to League One Burton Albion.

As his star continues to rise, Burrell is now excited about the next chapter in his football journey with the R's.

"I'm very proud and grateful to be here," Burrell said. "It's a great opportunity to showcase what I can do. It's a step up, but I'm ready.

"I feel having the experience and playing consistently, it has helped progress my game even further.

"I figured out areas of my game and was hell-bent on improving and trying to be the best version of me."

Burrell, who scored on his international debut in May against Trinidad, continued: "I can't wait to get in front of all the fans at Loftus Road."

KWAME POKU

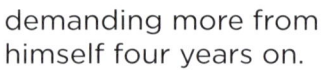

QPR were delighted to confirm the arrival of Kwame Poku, who joined from Peterborough United for an undisclosed fee.

The 23-year-old winger turned down numerous options to sign for the R's, and he explained: "I feel like the project they're building here excites me and I want to be part of taking QPR to that next level.

"There's good players here and I think it's exciting times for the club."

Poku spoke with new head coach Julien Stéphan ahead of putting pen to paper, and he admitted: "When I was speaking to him he was talking about where he sees me fitting in and where he thinks I can influence the game.

"That's what really attracted me. Being 23 turning 24, I'm not quite young anymore so I want to come in and make my mark from the jump."

Poku spent two years with Colchester United in League Two between 2019 and 2021, and he believes his time there, as well as his four years with the Posh, were crucial to his development.

"I think it was a journey that needed to happen to get me to this stage right now," he said.

"It was about being resilient and trying to be in a position where I can just showcase my talent every day and be the best version of myself."

During his time with Peterborough, Kwame developed a reputation for being an exciting prospect and now he wants to take the next step in his development.

He has already amassed more than 220 professional appearances despite his young age, something he is rightly proud of.

"I think that's a big part of my journey, being so young and playing a lot of games," he said.

"Going into this level, it's just about learning about this level, getting used to it and then expressing myself."

The Ghana international made 20 Championship appearances for Peterborough in 2019/20 so he knows what to expect – but he is demanding more from himself four years on.

"I think I had some good performances, good on the ball, I just think what separated then from now was the statistical side of it," he said.

"Coming into this team where there's a lot of good attacking players and good all-rounded players as well, I think I'll create more chances, be at the end of a lot of chances and get more numbers."

As he prepares for life with QPR, Poku added: "It's a new experience and I'm looking forward to it.

"I just want to get as many numbers individually as possible, and with the team improve on where we were last season.

"That's the main thing - carry on improving and see where it takes us."

RHYS NORRINGTON-DAVIES

Rhys Norrington-Davies joined QPR on a season-long loan from Sheffield United.

Left-back Norrington-Davies has been with the Blades since the age of 18. In the early days of his career, he enjoyed loan spells with Barrow and Rochdale. In 2020/21, meanwhile, he spent time on loan at both Luton Town and Stoke City - making 38 Championship appearances across the two clubs.

Having featured for Sheffield United 17 times last season, the 26-year-old is eager to achieve regular game-time with the R's.

"I'm looking forward to the opportunity to play for QPR," he said after completing the move.

"For me personally, I'm coming in here to play football."

Describing himself as a player, Norrington-Davies – who has represented Wales on 13 occasions – said: "I'd like to say I'm on the front foot, aggressive in nature, be that defensively or attacking. So now I'm looking forward to getting out there and showing the fans what I can do."

Norrington-Davies, who also featured in the Premier League for the Blades during 2023/24, joins a young Rangers group, and it is one he has a lot of belief in, adding: "The potential's there, there's some good names within the squad.

"It takes time for the whole squad to gel and it's still early days.

"Hopefully over the coming weeks and months, there'll be some positive performances and positive results."

KOKI SAITO

Koki Saito returned to QPR after completing a permanent transfer from Belgian side Lommel for an undisclosed fee.

The 24-year-old winger spent the duration of last season in W12 and became a firm fans' favourite for his energetic displays.

He made 42 appearances in all competitions, scoring three goals – and now he is eager for more.

Saito said: "I'm so happy. I'm so, so happy because I love QPR people.

"I am looking forward to playing. I want to make goals and assists. That is important for me and important for the team."

Saito admits his relationship with the QPR fans was a big factor for him as he considered his options, adding: "It's very important for me. When I played the game, when I received the ball, the fans sang my name. I love them.

"I'm really looking forward to wearing this (QPR) shirt and seeing the fans."

KEALEY ADAMSON

Defender Kealey Adamson completed a permanent transfer to QPR from Australian A-League side Macarthur FC, for an undisclosed fee.

Adamson, who was an ever-present for the Bulls in 2024/25, said: "I'm super excited.

"QPR is a massive club and an old club with lots of history. Even in Australia, I feel everyone knows who QPR is. It's a really attractive club, really well supported and the list goes on.

"I'm just keen to hit the ground running and get to work."

While Adamson was already excited at the prospect of joining the R's, he admits a conversation with Macarthur centre-back Ollie Jones also helped his decision making.

"He's a massive QPR fan," Adamson explained. "I was keeping up to date with the results even before I knew there was any interest because he would just come into the changing room watching the end of games, watching highlights, so I feel like really there was a connection without me even knowing it.

"I told him a little bit about the interest and he goes: 'You're going, you're going, you're going!'

"He was very excited."

Adamson moved into professional football three years ago when he joined Sydney FC, initially representing their U21s in Australia's second tier.

He made 19 league starts and such was his form that he progressed to play for the senior side in the Australia Cup, helping them lift the trophy with a 3-1 win against Brisbane Roar at the end of 2023.

Before the turn of the year, Adamson joined Macarthur FC – and in his first season with his new side he repeated his Australia Cup success, this time lifting the trophy after a 1-0 win over Melbourne Victory.

He also made 13 A-League appearances, including a Finals outing. By 2024/25, Adamson was a regular, scoring twice in 26 appearances.

Describing himself as a player, Adamson explained: "I like to think I'm a very modern right-back.

"I'm lucky I've got an engine, I've got pace to be able to get forward, join the attack a lot when I can and still be able to come back and be disciplined in defence.

"So I feel that work-rate is the biggest thing you're going to get. I'm going to be at both ends of the pitch and hopefully you'll be seeing two of me on the field!"

On the international stage, Adamson has represented Australia at U23 level, and he is aiming to continue his development at QPR, where he has already been impressed.

Adamson said: "I'd heard a lot of good things from afar, but I think since having touched down, seeing the facilities, meeting the staff, meeting all the support network around the first team, I think it's just super clear to see how I'll be able to grow my game and how other players have grown their game in the past."

ISAAC HAYDEN

Isaac Hayden returned to QPR on a free transfer following his departure from Newcastle United.

The 30-year-old midfielder spent four months in W12 at the end of the 2023/24 campaign and he is delighted to be back.

"It's fantastic," he said. "It was special to have the conversation with Christian (Nourry) and the head coach (Julien Stéphan) in terms of them wanting me back at the club.

"I had a few options to go abroad, but it was one of those where if I was going to stay in the Championship, it was only going to be one club and I'm just glad to get it done."

Hayden, who spent the second half of last season on loan at Portsmouth, admits his previous spell with Rangers left an impact on him, and he is keen to use his experience to help the R's squad.

"Last year when I was at Portsmouth, it was quite difficult to play against the guys," he said. "I felt like I was lining up on the wrong team!

"It was a special four months that I had at the club and you get a feeling sometimes of a place that is kind of like home. And it was just one of those situations where, for me, it was a no-brainer to come back.

"I feel like I can add a lot of value, not just on the pitch, but off the pitch as well and help drive the group forward."

While keen to use his experience in the dressing room, the Jamaica international is also determined to make his mark on the pitch.

"This year especially for me is a big one," he said.

"With Jamaica we've got the potential for a World Cup at the end of the season, six massive games to try and qualify. But obviously for me to play for them, I need to be playing football at a good level.

"I want to try and play as much as possible. Everyone thinks you hit the big 3-0 and it's downhill from there. But I do feel like I've got so much more in me."

Hayden also had a special word for the QPR fans, adding: "I want to say thank you so much for the support. It means the world to me to feel wanted and to feel valued.

"I think they know what they're going to get from me, 110%, giving everything for the shirt on and off the pitch."

THE NEWBIES

DEFENDER

LIAM
MORRISON

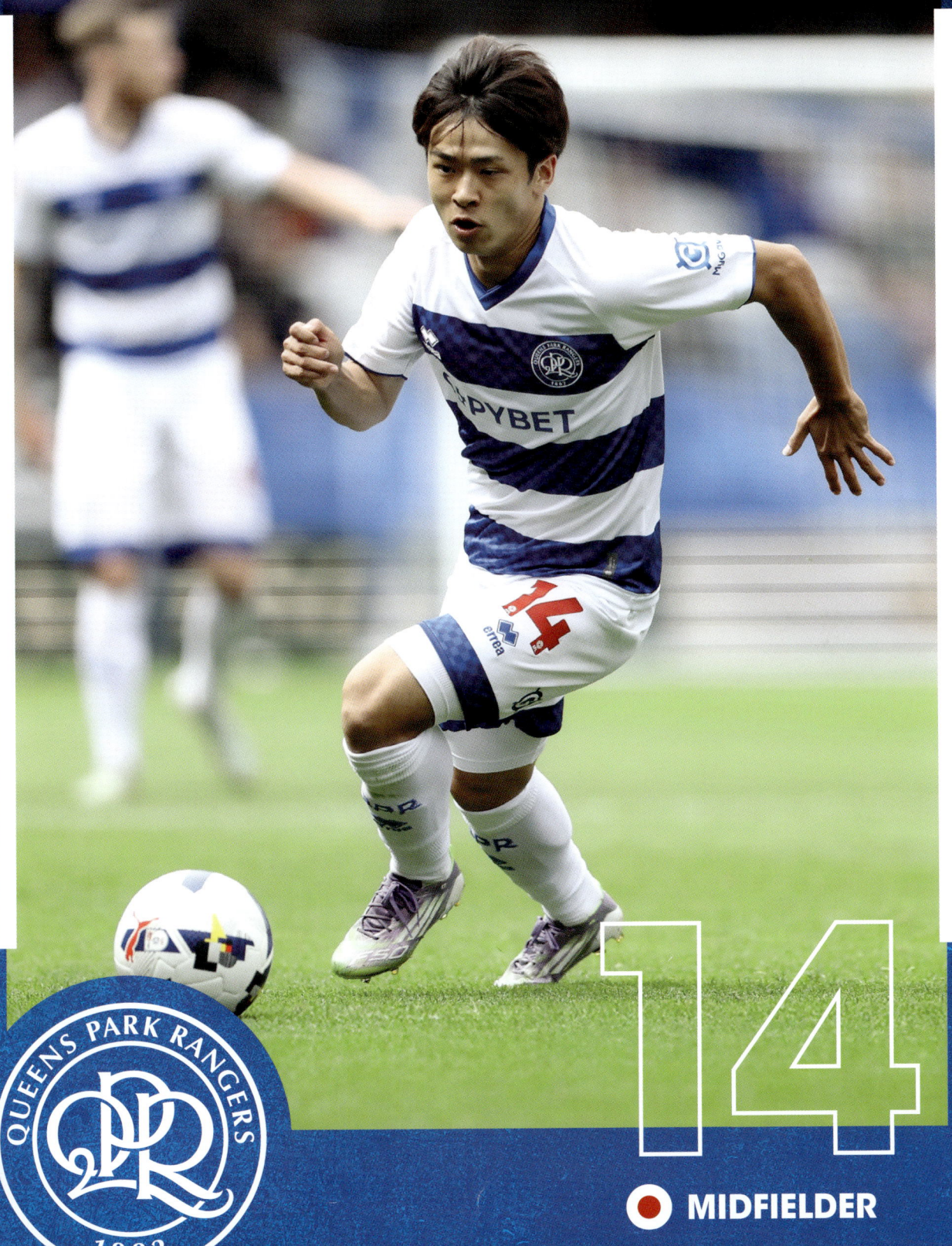

MIDFIELDER

KOKI SAITO

JIMMY'S CLEAN SWEEP

PLAYER AWARDS 2024/25

QPR defender Jimmy Dunne was voted the MyGuava Supporters' Player of the Year for the 2024/25 campaign.

A virtual ever-present in Rangers' backline last term, Dunne scooped three awards in total following a season which saw him win a first senior cap for the Republic of Ireland.

Jimmy also took the Ray Jones Players' Player of the Year and Achilleus Security Junior Hoops Player of the Year awards.

Elsewhere, Southampton loanee **Ronnie Edwards** was your **Daphne Biggs** Young Player of the Year following his own impressive displays after switching from St Mary's in January - while **Paul Smyth's** incredible long-range strike at Bristol City in December was the Kiyan Prince Goal of the Season.

Supporters were able to select their NNR QPR FC Women's Player of the Year, too, with striker **Grace Stanley** yet again topping the vote.

Alfie Lloyd and **Chloe Sampson** were our PFA Community Champions of the Year for supporting numerous club and Community Trust events and projects.

And finally, **Declan Finnegan** was named QPR Supporter of the Year - as voted for by fellow fans.

Proud Irishman Declan has been following club and country for over 50 years, both home and away, with his Irish R's flag on display at stadiums across the globe.

Declan is a big part of the Irish R's Facebook community, acting as a go-between for many of our supporters from the Emerald Isle. The group boasts more than 1,000 members, lots of whom meet at 'Irish Corner' in the Coningham Arms, Uxbridge Road on matchdays.

ROLL OF HONOUR

MyGuava Supporters' POTY
Jimmy Dunne (Runner-up: Paul Nardi)

Ray Jones Players' POTY
Jimmy Dunne (Runner-up: Sam Field)

Daphne Biggs Young POTY
Ronnie Edwards (Runner-up: Koki Saito)

Achilleus Security Junior Hoops POTY
Jimmy Dunne (Runner-up: Koki Saito)

Kiyan Prince Goal of the Season
Paul Smyth v Bristol City (A)
(Runner-up: Koki Saito v Hull City (A))

NNR QPR FC Women's POTY
Grace Stanley (Runner-up: Jess Cooper)

PFA Men's Community
Champion of the Year **Alfie Lloyd**

PFA Women's Community
Champion of the Year **Chloe Sampson**

QPR Supporter of the Year
Declan Finnegan

CONGRATULATIONS TO ALL OUR WINNERS.

The awards were presented pitchside shortly before our final home fixture of the campaign.

FOCUS ON

NATIONALITY: Danish

POSITION: Midfielder

MARRIED: No

CHILDREN: No

CAR: None – Jimmy Dunne is my driver!

FAVOURITE TV PROGRAMME: Ted Lasso

FAVOURITE PLAYER IN WORLD FOOTBALL: Virgil van Dijk

MOST PROMISING TEAM-MATE: Ilias Chair

FAVOURITE MEAL: Spaghetti bolognese

FAVOURITE HOLIDAY DESTINATION: Spain

FAVOURITE PERSONALITY (I.E. COMEDIAN, ACTOR): Rafael Nadal

FAVOURITE ACTIVITY ON DAY OFF: Play padel or get a good coffee

FAVOURITE MUSICIAN / BAND: Disclosure

POST-MATCH ROUTINE: Go home, eat a big portion of spaghetti bolognese and some sweets!

NICOLAS MADSEN

FAVOURITE TEAM APART FROM QPR: Liverpool

CHILDHOOD FOOTBALLING HERO: Steven Gerrard

FAVOURITE SPORT OTHER THAN FOOTBALL: Tennis

MOST DIFFICULT OPPONENT SO FAR (PLAYER): Mo Salah

MOST MEMORABLE MATCH OF YOUR CAREER: Playing in the Champions League against Liverpool

BIGGEST DISAPPOINTMENT IN FOOTBALL SO FAR: I don't have one

BEST FRIEND IN FOOTBALL: Anders Dreyer (San Diego)

BIGGEST CAREER INFLUENCE: My parents, my brother and my agent/friend

PERSONAL LIFE AMBITION: To enjoy it and be happy

IF YOU WEREN'T A FOOTBALLER, WHAT WOULD YOU BE: Football scout

PERSON IN WORLD YOU'D MOST LIKE TO MEET: Jürgen Klopp

YOU ARE THE REF

01

A player is about to take a penalty kick but as he runs up to strike the ball an opposing player shouts, "miss!", and subsequently the penalty taker's shot does miss the goal. After you have cautioned the defending player **what action do you take?**

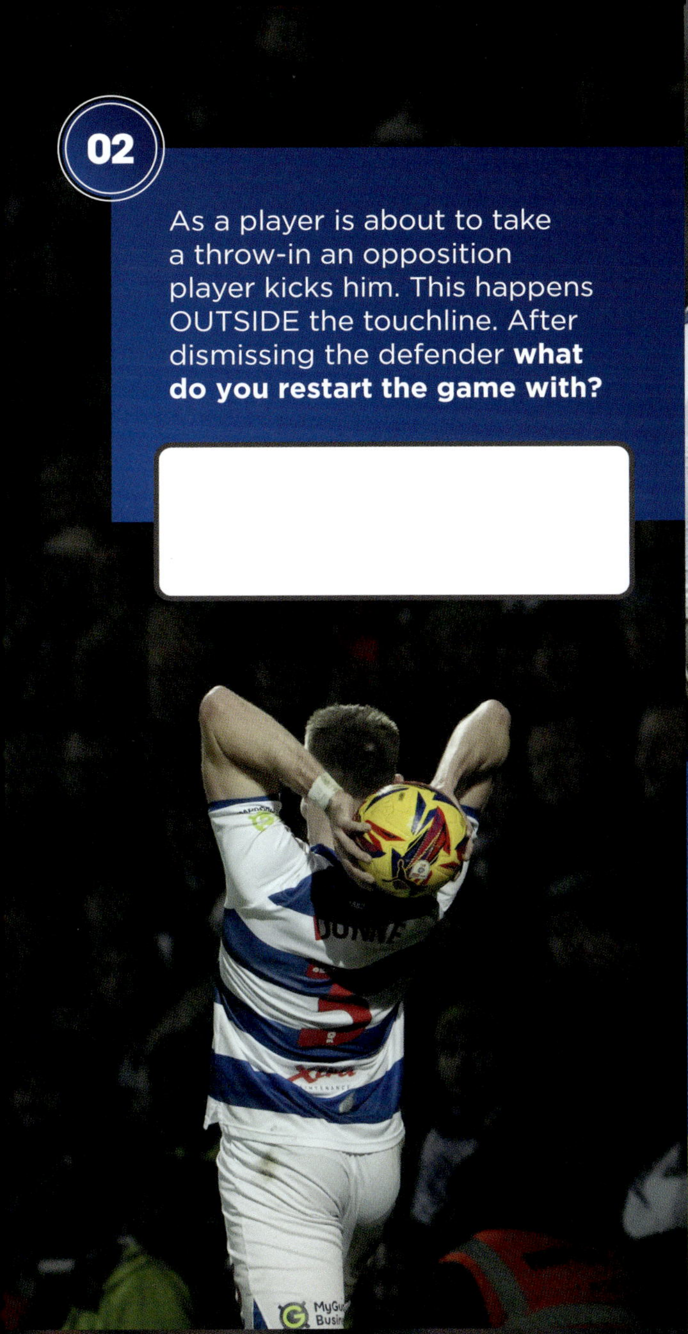

02

As a player is about to take a throw-in an opposition player kicks him. This happens OUTSIDE the touchline. After dismissing the defender **what do you restart the game with?**

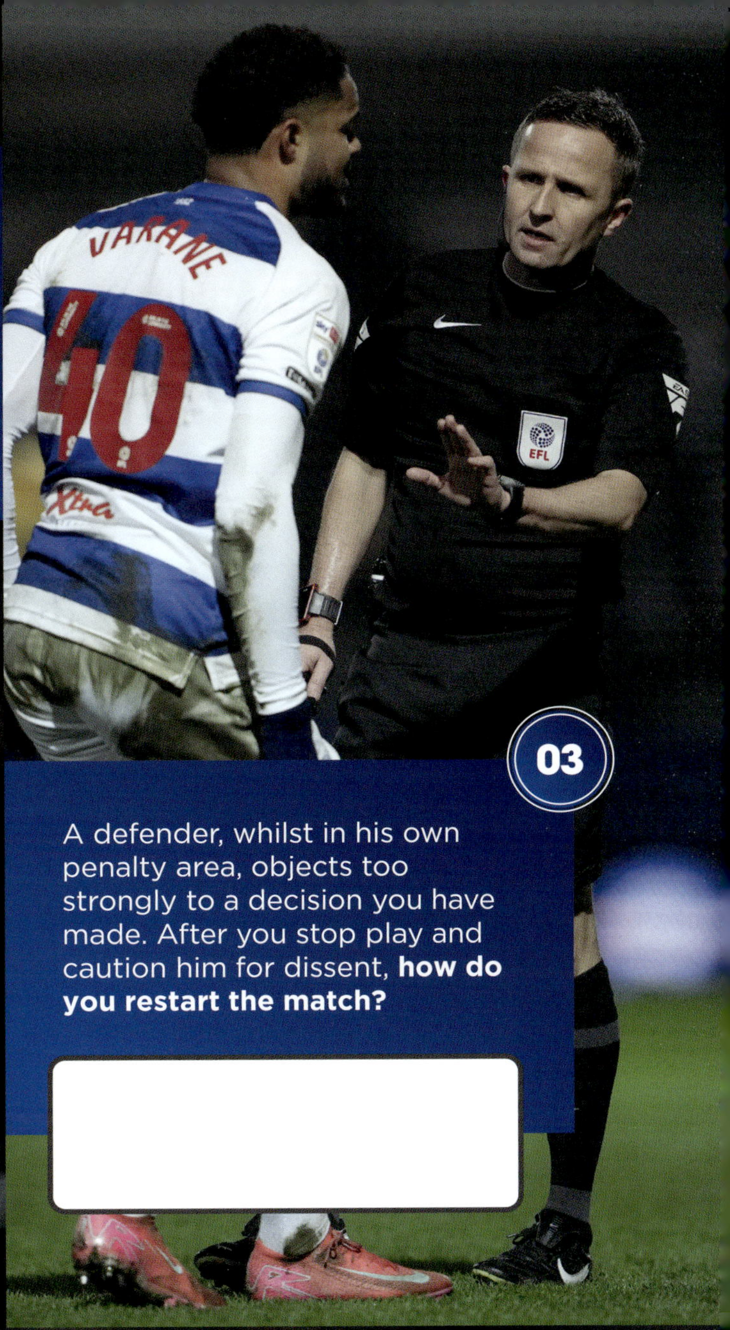

03

A defender, whilst in his own penalty area, objects too strongly to a decision you have made. After you stop play and caution him for dissent, **how do you restart the match?**

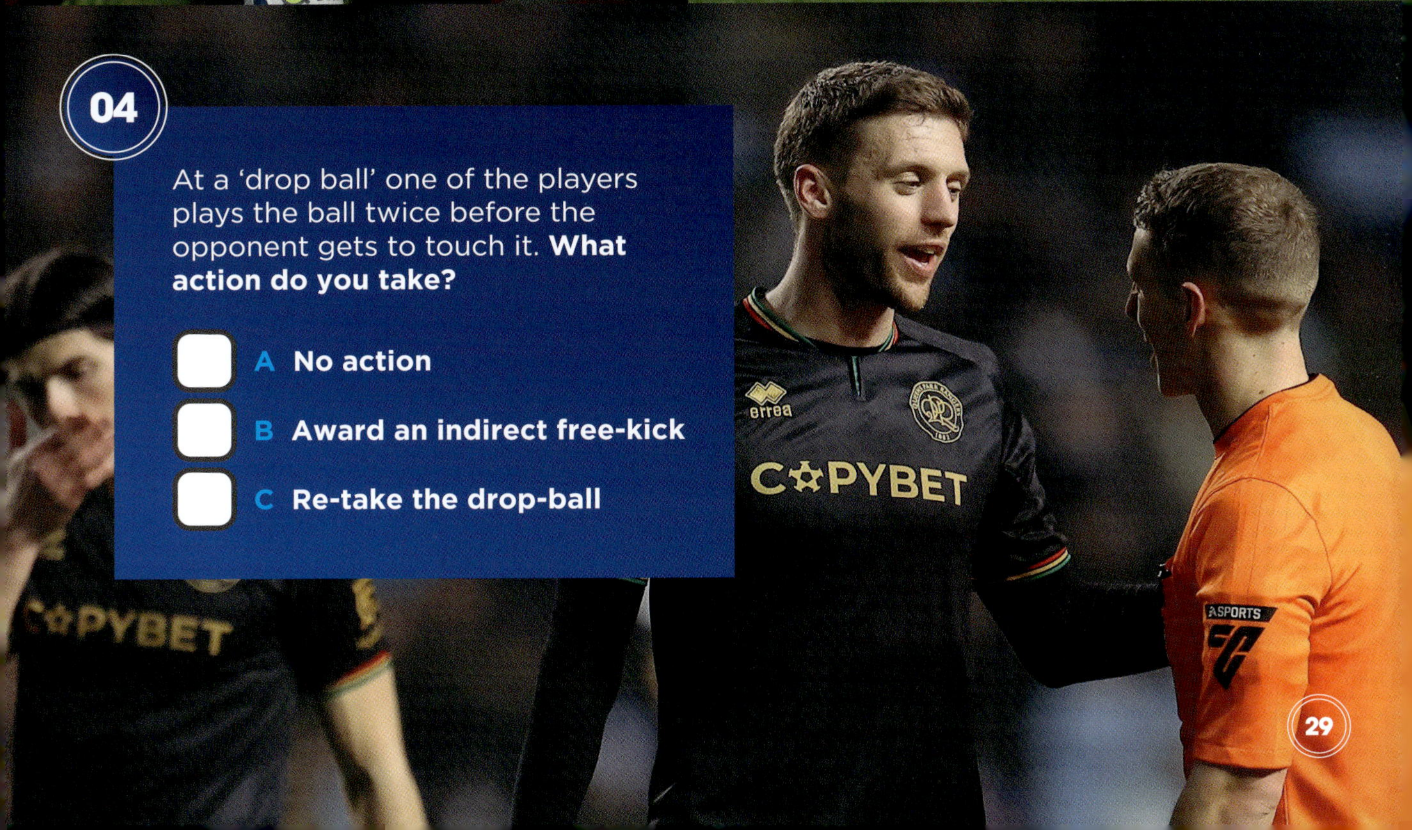

04

At a 'drop ball' one of the players plays the ball twice before the opponent gets to touch it. **What action do you take?**

- [ ] **A** No action
- [ ] **B** Award an indirect free-kick
- [ ] **C** Re-take the drop-ball

05

With five minutes of full time remaining really bad fog descends. The score is 3-0. **What should you do?**

- [ ] A Abandon the match
- [ ] B Wait in the hope that the fog clears
- [ ] C Award the match to the leading team

06

At another 'drop-ball' situation a player kicks wildly, misses the ball and strikes the opponent quite hard. **What do you do?**

- [ ] A Take no action
- [ ] B Award a free-kick
- [ ] C Re-take the drop-ball

07

You are booking a player who then refuses to give you his name. **What is your next action?**

- [ ] A Just note his number
- [ ] B Send him off

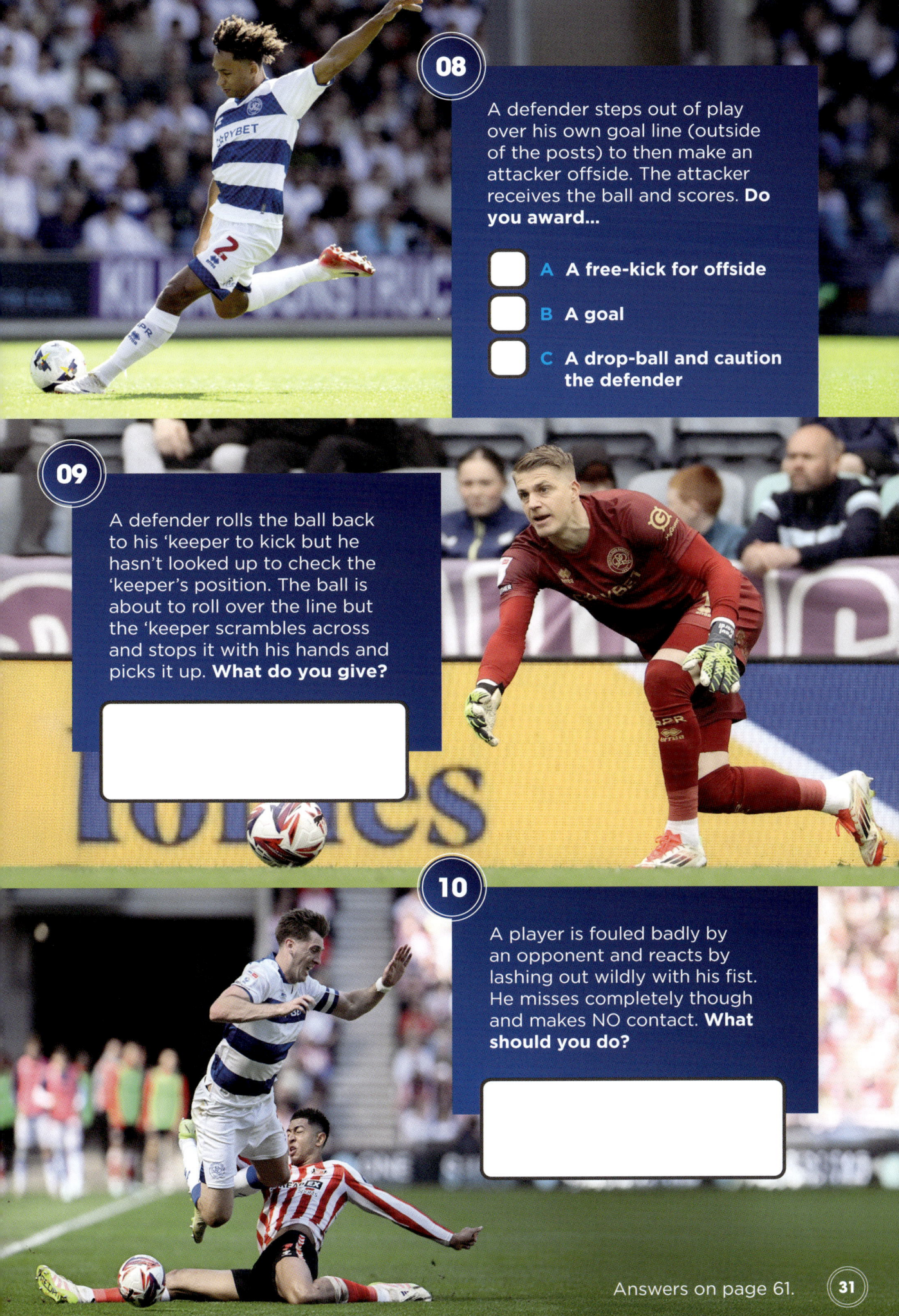

08

A defender steps out of play over his own goal line (outside of the posts) to then make an attacker offside. The attacker receives the ball and scores. **Do you award...**

- A A free-kick for offside
- B A goal
- C A drop-ball and caution the defender

09

A defender rolls the ball back to his 'keeper to kick but he hasn't looked up to check the 'keeper's position. The ball is about to roll over the line but the 'keeper scrambles across and stops it with his hands and picks it up. **What do you give?**

10

A player is fouled badly by an opponent and reacts by lashing out wildly with his fist. He misses completely though and makes NO contact. **What should you do?**

Answers on page 61.

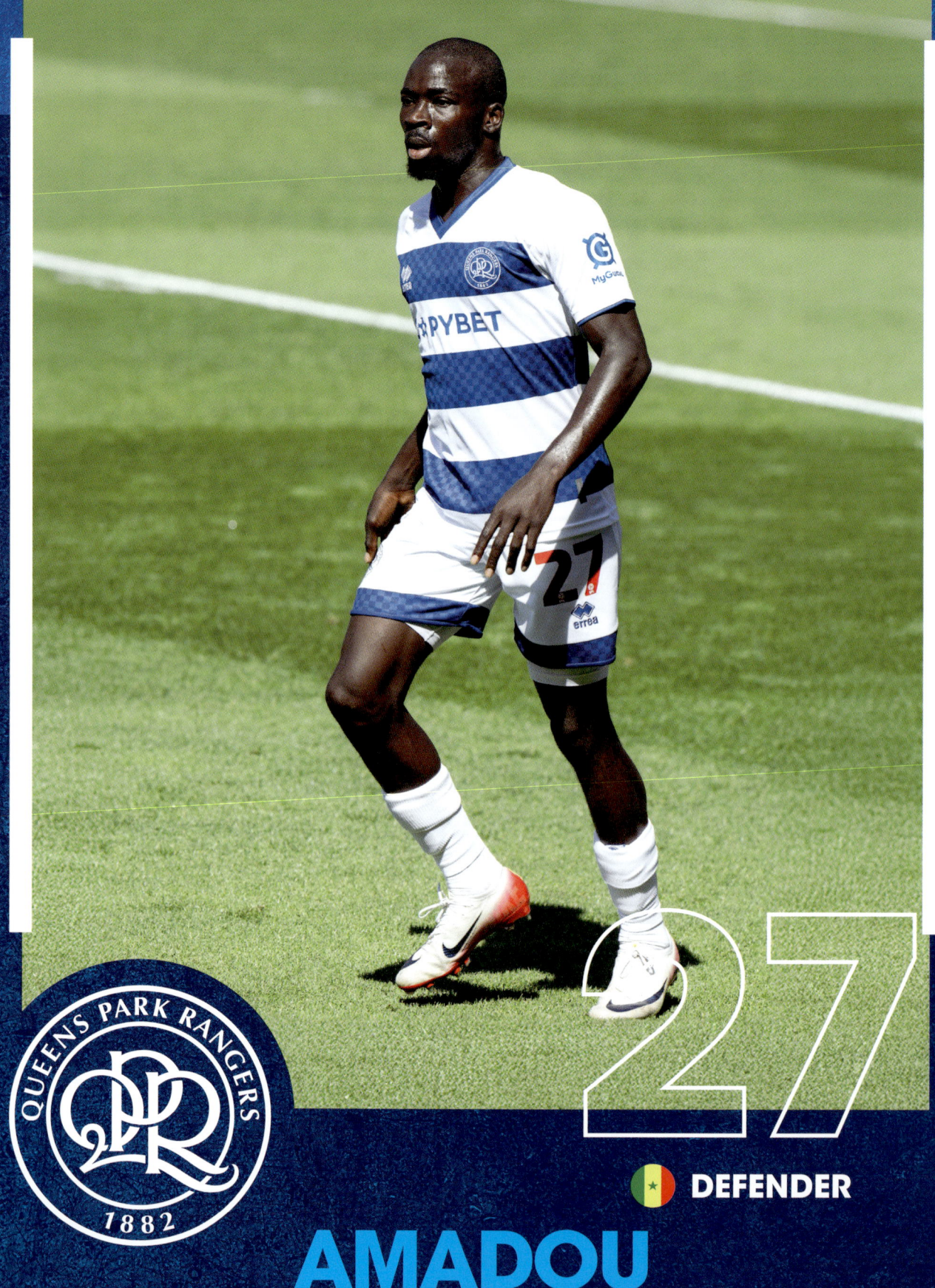

AMADOU MBENGUE

27 — DEFENDER

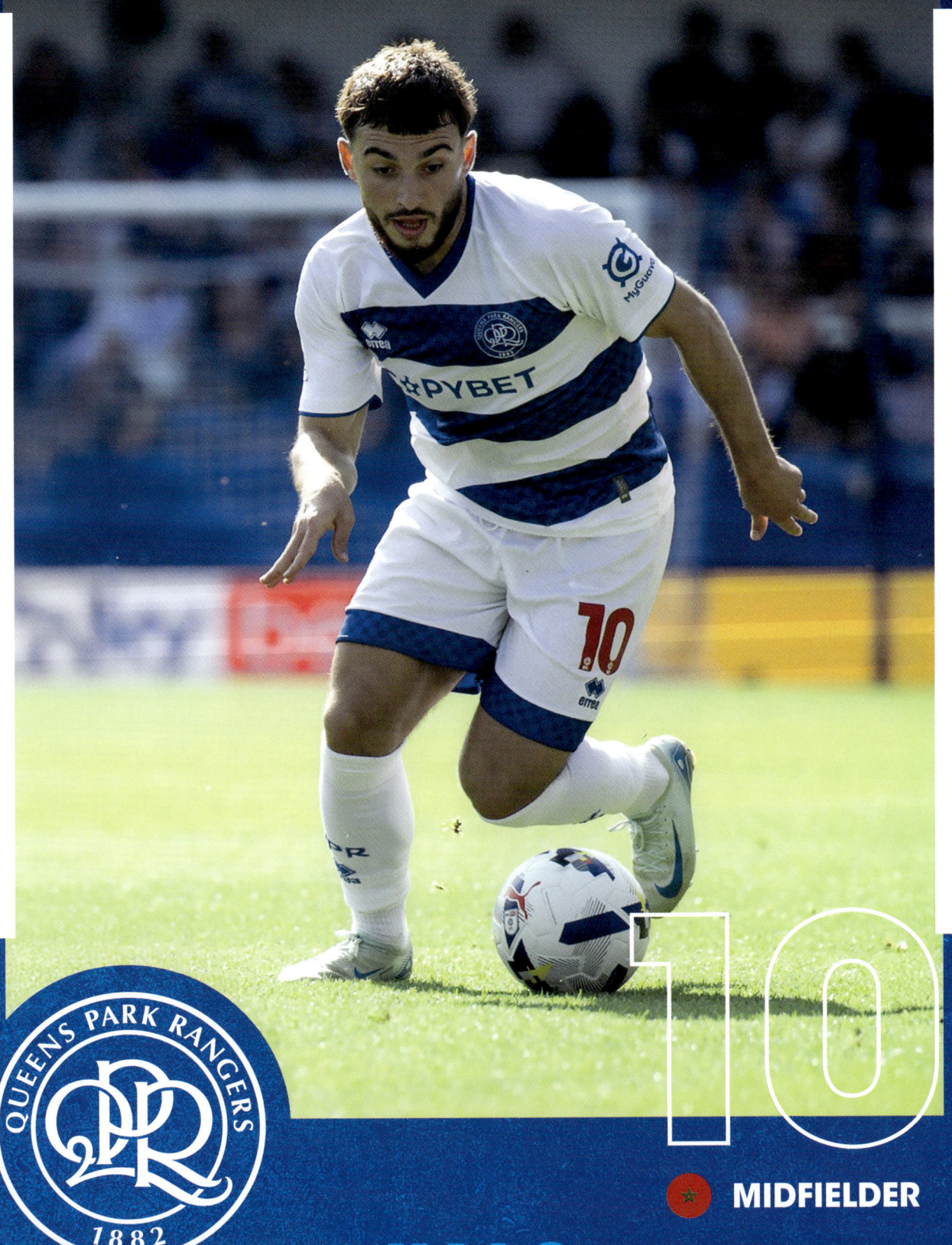

ILIAS CHAIR

10 — MIDFIELDER

THE STORY OF 1975/76

WRITTEN BY FRANCIS ATKINSON

Fifty years on from QPR's famous title challenge of 1975/76, we look back on a campaign that so nearly yielded top-flight glory for the R's...

Parkes, Clement, Gillard, Hollins, McLintock, Webb, Thomas, Francis, Masson, Bowles, Givens. Sub: Leach.

A QPR side that picked itself and rarely altered over the course of an arduous 42-match, top-flight league campaign. Managed by Dave Sexton, the R's had spent two years (since their promotion to the top flight of English football in 1973) building a strong squad full of talent and experience, and they were finally ready to announce themselves as one of the most attractive, skilful and entertaining teams in the country.

QPR began the season superbly by beating eventual champions Liverpool convincingly on the opening day, the 2-0 scoreline flattering the Merseysiders, with the opening goal by Gerry Francis winning 'Goal of the Season' that year. It was a superb team goal and epitomised the free-flowing football that was the hallmark of Sexton's Rangers.

The R's followed that up by thumping reigning champions Derby County 5-1 on their own turf, with Stan Bowles grabbing a hat-trick, and that was swiftly followed by a solid win over a very strong Manchester United. QPR had arrived and their title intentions were there for all to see from the start.

It was after 11 games that the team lost for the first time in a narrow 2-1 defeat at a hostile Leeds United, but Rangers bounced back immediately by smashing Everton 5-0. With a team full of internationals playing a continental style, confident, exciting football, it was hard to see Rangers faltering - but falter they did over the New Year period, losing four matches out of six.

The heavy pitches and poor weather seemingly hampered Rangers' style of play as the team slipped to fifth. However, at the end of January, a 2-0 away victory at Aston Villa started an incredible run of 11 straight wins which sent QPR top by the end of April, a point ahead of Liverpool with three matches to play.

An agonising 3-2 defeat at Norwich City (with a clear offside goal helping win it for the Canaries on the day) handed the advantage back to Liverpool. Both teams won their penultimate fixtures and so it was that QPR faced a great Leeds United team at a packed Loftus Road (31,002 the recorded crowd) on April 24th 1976.

1975–76 TOP LEAGUE GOAL SCORERS

DON GIVENS
13 GOALS

GERRY FRANCIS
12 GOALS

STAN BOWLES
10 GOALS

DON MASSON
6 GOALS

DAVID WEBB
5 GOALS

A nervous home crowd witnessed a deserved 2-0 win that day which saw the Super Hoops finish top of the table, leading Liverpool by a single point. The Reds then had 10 days before their final game against relegation-threatened Wolverhampton Wanderers - an unfair advantage that certainly wouldn't happen nowadays.

Wolves incredibly led 1-0 until the last 15 minutes but succumbed 3-1 on the night and the title went to Liverpool, QPR ending an incredible season as runners-up by a solitary point.

A tragedy as this team was undoubtedly the best-ever Rangers side and arguably the best team in the country at the time. The boys from west London had still qualified for Europe - a tremendous achievement - and the disappointment of losing the title certainly wasn't evident in the European campaign the following season as the R's put some of Europe's top sides to the sword.

A repeat of the league title challenge didn't materialise, though, due largely to key injuries and fixture congestion, and QPR supporters could only look on and ponder 'what might have been', had our greatest-ever team not lost at Norwich!

1975-76 FIRST DIVISION RESULTS

Date	Opponent	H/A	Result
16 Aug 1975	Liverpool	H	2-0
19 Aug 1975	Aston Villa	H	1-1
23 Aug 1975	Derby County	A	5-1
26 Aug 1975	Wolves	A	2-2
30 Aug 1975	West Ham United	H	1-1
06 Sep 1975	Birmingham City	A	1-1
13 Sep 1975	Manchester United	H	1-0
20 Sep 1975	Middlesbrough	A	0-0
23 Sep 1975	Leicester City	H	1-0
27 Sep 1975	Newcastle United	H	1-0
04 Oct 1975	Leeds United	A	1-2
11 Oct 1975	Everton	H	5-0
18 Oct 1975	Stoke City	H	3-2
25 Oct 1975	Manchester City	A	0-1
01 Nov 1975	Sheffield United	H	3-0
08 Nov 1975	Ipswich Town	A	0-2
15 Nov 1975	Tottenham Hotspur	H	1-1
22 Nov 1975	Arsenal	A	0-1
29 Nov 1975	Coventry City	H	3-0
06 Dec 1975	Burnley	A	1-3
13 Dec 1975	Norwich City	H	1-0
20 Dec 1975	West Ham United	A	1-2
26 Dec 1975	Birmingham City	H	2-0
27 Dec 1975	Liverpool	A	2-3
03 Jan 1976	Aston Villa	A	1-3
17 Jan 1976	Derby County	H	0-0
24 Jan 1976	Leicester City	A	1-0
31 Jan 1976	Aston Villa	A	2-0
14 Feb 1976	Tottenham Hotspur	A	2-0
21 Feb 1976	Ipswich Town	H	4-1
28 Feb 1976	Arsenal	H	2-1
06 Mar 1976	Sheffield United	A	2-0
13 Mar 1976	Coventry City	A	1-0
16 Mar 1976	Burnley	H	1-0
20 Mar 1976	Norwich City	A	3-1
23 Mar 1976	Wolves	H	1-0
27 Mar 1976	Leeds United	H	2-0
03 Apr 1976	Everton	A	1-1
06 Apr 1976	Manchester City	H	1-0
10 Apr 1976	Middlesbrough	H	4-2
17 Apr 1976	Norwich City	A	2-3
19 Apr 1976	Arsenal	H	2-1
24 Apr 1976	Leeds United	H	2-0

GOALS

MICHAEL FREY
v Luton Town (A)

1

GOALS from Nicolas Madsen and Michael Frey saw QPR come from behind to earn a first league win of the season against Luton Town in late August.

After falling behind to Jimmy Dunne's 18th-minute own goal and having to soak up plenty of subsequent home pressure in the first half, Rangers battled back after half-time to claim three excellent points against the Hatters.

Madsen's first goal for the club on 69 minutes owed much to the perseverance of team-mate Frey – before the frontman got in on the scoring act just three minutes later when meeting Kenneth Paal's cross.

ALFIE LLOYD
v Sheffield Wednesday (A)

2

QPR sealed an INSANE point at Sheffield Wednesday after they looked to have suffered injury-time heartache at Hillsborough.

After a real battle, the game looked to be heading for a goalless draw before Barry Bannan appeared to have snatched maximum points for the Owls with a 93rd-minute half-volley.

While the home fans celebrated what was set to be their first win since the opening day, late substitute Alfie Lloyd scored his first goal for the club on 96 minutes, sparking scenes of absolute delirium among the away fans.

With one final corner, there was the most incredible goalmouth scramble. Bodies were flying everywhere. The ref allowed it to continue, and suddenly the ball was smashed into the back of the Wednesday net.

It was Lloyd who wheeled away. My word.

24/25

3 KADER DEMBELE
v Portsmouth (H)

RANGERS' search for a first home league win of the season went into October following a 2-1 defeat to Portsmouth at MATRADE Loftus Road.

The R's had led in W12 after Kader Dembele caught visiting goalkeeper Nicolas Schmid off his line with an impressive lobbed finish in the ninth minute.

But League One champions Pompey bounced back to collect their first Championship win of the campaign.

Freddie Potts' 18th-minute strike restored parity for the visitors who then went one better in the second half, with Callum Lang's 57th-minute penalty proving decisive for John Mousinho's charges.

4 KIERAN MORGAN
v Coventry City (H)

KIERAN Morgan's first-ever professional goal rescued a point for Rangers against Coventry City later that month.

The 18-year-old – who joined QPR from Tottenham Hotspur in the summer and was making just his second-ever league appearance – struck in the 63rd minute, just five minutes after his introduction.

Earlier, Haji Wright had given Coventry a fourth-minute lead. The 1-1 draw was probably a fair outcome on the balance of play.

5 ŽAN CELAR
Cardiff City (A)

THEY say a week is a long time in football. Try four days. From the low of his penalty miss against Stoke on the Saturday, to the high of being a match-winning, brace-getting hero; Žan Celar showed R's fans what he is capable of with two very different goals, both of them stunning, as QPR picked up a crucial 2-0 win at Cardiff City.

His first came in the 40th minute as he crashed a half-volley into the top corner, shaking off the attention of three Cardiff defenders as he did so.

The second wrapped up the win in injury time and was the cherry on the cake.

After a determined rear-guard performance to hold onto our one-goal lead, Harrison Ashby played Celar in with a ball over the top.

Celar had time – and oh, how he used it, nonchalantly getting his second of the night to seal a big, big win.

6 PAUL SMYTH
v Bristol City (A)
GOAL OF THE SEASON

QPR came from behind to earn a 1-1 draw at Bristol City, and in doing so extend their unbeaten run to six matches shortly before Christmas.

The Robins took the lead on the hour mark at Ashton Gate with an excellent free-kick from Scott Twine, but Rangers weren't going to give up the points that easily – and it was Paul Smyth who ensured a share of the spoils with a stunning long-range strike to open his league account for the campaign. After skipping past the out-rushing home goalkeeper, Smyth took aim from distance and dropped the ball brilliantly into the open goal on 65 minutes.

It led to scenes of delight among the travelling fans at that end of the pitch and was a great point to add to the week's earlier collection of six.

7 JONATHAN VARANE
v Leicester City (A)

RANGERS' involvement in last season's Emirates FA Cup started and ended against Premier League Leicester City in the third round, who ran out 6-2 winners in an entertaining spectacle at King Power Stadium.

Jonathan Varane's first-ever professional goal (18 minutes) cancelled out James Justin's eighth-minute opener, while Rayan Kolli was also on target moments before half-time.

But it wasn't to be for the R's, ultimately, with Stephy Mavididi (35), Facundo Buonanotte (38), Jamie Vardy (51), Justin again (63) and Wout Faes (90+3) also on the scoresheet for the Foxes.

8

RAYAN KOLLI
v Plymouth Argyle (A)

RAYAN Kolli came from the bench to score a second-half winner for QPR, who beat Plymouth Argyle 1-0 in January.

Fresh from signing a new long-term contract on the Friday, Kolli netted in the 65th minute - just six minutes after coming on - to earn the R's all three points at Home Park.

A third consecutive league success was no more than Rangers deserved after also spurning several other excellent opportunities during this lunchtime kick-off.

9

KOKI SAITO
v Hull City (A)

QPR made it four wins in a row with a thoroughly-deserved 2-1 win at Hull City.

Second-half goals from Kenneth Paal and Koki Saito seemingly gave QPR control of the game but there had to be a bit of late drama to keep the nerves jangling!

Rangers never really looked in danger of losing this one. After an even first half, two goals in six minutes put QPR in control, firstly from Paal and then a cracking solo effort from substitute Saito.

It looked as if the game was fizzling out for a relatively-comfortable win but a great goal from Joseph Gelhardt on 84 minutes made it a nervous finish. Rangers held firm, however.

10

LUCAS ANDERSEN
v Preston North End (A)

GOALS from Michi Frey and Lucas Andersen saw Rangers come from behind to deservedly beat Preston North End on Good Friday.

After QPR trailed to Liam Lindsay's header in first-half stoppage time, the R's eventually responded late on to claim all three points.

Frey lashed home in the 80th minute - just four minutes after being introduced - eventually taking control of fellow substitute Andersen's ball into the penalty area.

The scene was then set for Andersen to finish the job, and in some style!

The Dane, who had been on the pitch 15 minutes, intercepted a loose pass 25 yards from goal. Gifted time to take a touch and pick his spot, that's precisely what he did, arrowing a stunning strike into the top corner that led to special scenes in front of the travelling QPR supporters.

FOCUS ON

HARVEY VALE

NATIONALITY: English

POSITION: Midfielder

MARRIED: No

CHILDREN: No

CAR: Mercedes

FAVOURITE TV PROGRAMME: Power

FAVOURITE PLAYER IN WORLD FOOTBALL: Kevin De Bruyne

MOST PROMISING TEAM-MATE: Liam Morrison

FAVOURITE MEAL: Anything with steak!

FAVOURITE HOLIDAY DESTINATION: Ibiza

FAVOURITE PERSONALITY (I.E. COMEDIAN, ACTOR): Tom Cruise

FAVOURITE ACTIVITY ON DAY OFF: Chill with my dog

FAVOURITE MUSICIAN / BAND: Coldplay

POST-MATCH ROUTINE: Eat! Then watch TV

BEST FRIEND IN FOOTBALL: Alfie Gilchrist

FAVOURITE TEAM APART FROM QPR: West Ham

CHILDHOOD FOOTBALLING HERO: Wayne Rooney

FAVOURITE SPORT OTHER THAN FOOTBALL: Golf

MOST DIFFICULT OPPONENT SO FAR (PLAYER): Harry Kane

MOST MEMORABLE MATCH OF YOUR CAREER: U19s Euros Final win with England

BIGGEST DISAPPOINTMENT IN FOOTBALL SO FAR: Being injured when I signed in January

BIGGEST CAREER INFLUENCE: Thomas Tuchel

PERSONAL LIFE AMBITION: Play as many times as possible in the Premier League

IF YOU WEREN'T A FOOTBALLER, WHAT WOULD YOU BE: Golfer

PERSON IN WORLD YOU'D MOST LIKE TO MEET: Lionel Messi

THE FINEST FOOTBALL TEAM

50 years ago, arguably our finest ever football team were taking the top tier of English soccer by storm. They swept aside most of who they encountered with a swashbuckling style of football rarely seen back in the day. A multi-talented squad and forward-thinking manager that were denied the ultimate prize by a single point.

Can you find all of the player names, plus the manager, hidden within the wordsearch? Answers on page 61.

```
Y W A J H F J V H A T A C Z V F B C I F K W
O Q M D D Z R O M S G H H Q I Q F V N F Y K
F H F Z Y N L A L T N T N S M T M X I Q A H
W A U E I L D B N L T U E E G J A E E A K C
N E J D I V K R U C T P C K E E M U T N S A
K O Q N C Q P J A T I C Z R Y K J A O C S E
F O S Q P T A G G L Y S L A T H T T S Z T L
E R K E V O L H S B L K D P I E X P V S G B
H Z X C I J G S K K D I E L F E K D J E O U
F X D Z O U K Z N W T L G T S A V E O P Z N
R U E A J T B N A E L K M U N J U M I P A S
T K S Q D X N G H P O D Z C C E W Q H D R X
O U X O D F W I S S W J C Z W U M W A K D I
C O F S Z C D U L O N R H P F Q E E E G A W
U H S Y E N R Q O C A R J V B B G H L T S P
D M O H R L J E Y S M B W S B W N N H C E Z
W V G F E I W T Q O N T E K R C Q O C H C D
B I J I T J E O O Q T Q B C N W M H W L Z B
M V I A V J O J B O K E Z U K A C G L V X A
I T V Z I E X I B I J S F J S T S O U F V K
V Q Y W H N N B W R J M Q B P G L L E L G W
P E L Z F Q A S V E X R W T G G R W L O U B
```

Sexton	**Hollins**	**Masson**	**Abbott**
Parkes	**McLintock**	**Bowles**	**Nutt**
Clement	**Webb**	**Givens**	**Beck**
Gillard	**Thomas**	**Leach**	**Tagg**
	Francis	**Shanks**	

GUESS THE PLAYERS

We've jumbled up the faces of some of your R's stars.
Can you work out which three players have created each face?

Answers on page 61.

1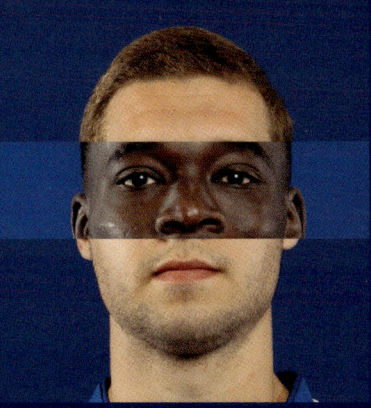

| HEAD |
| EYES |
| MOUTH |

2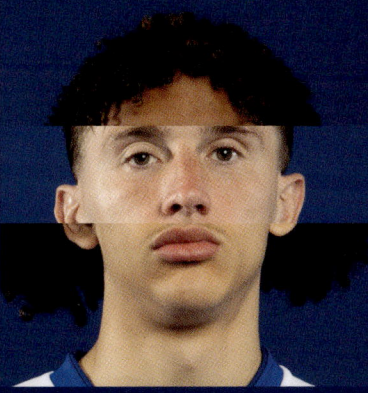

| HEAD |
| EYES |
| MOUTH |

3

| HEAD |
| EYES |
| MOUTH |

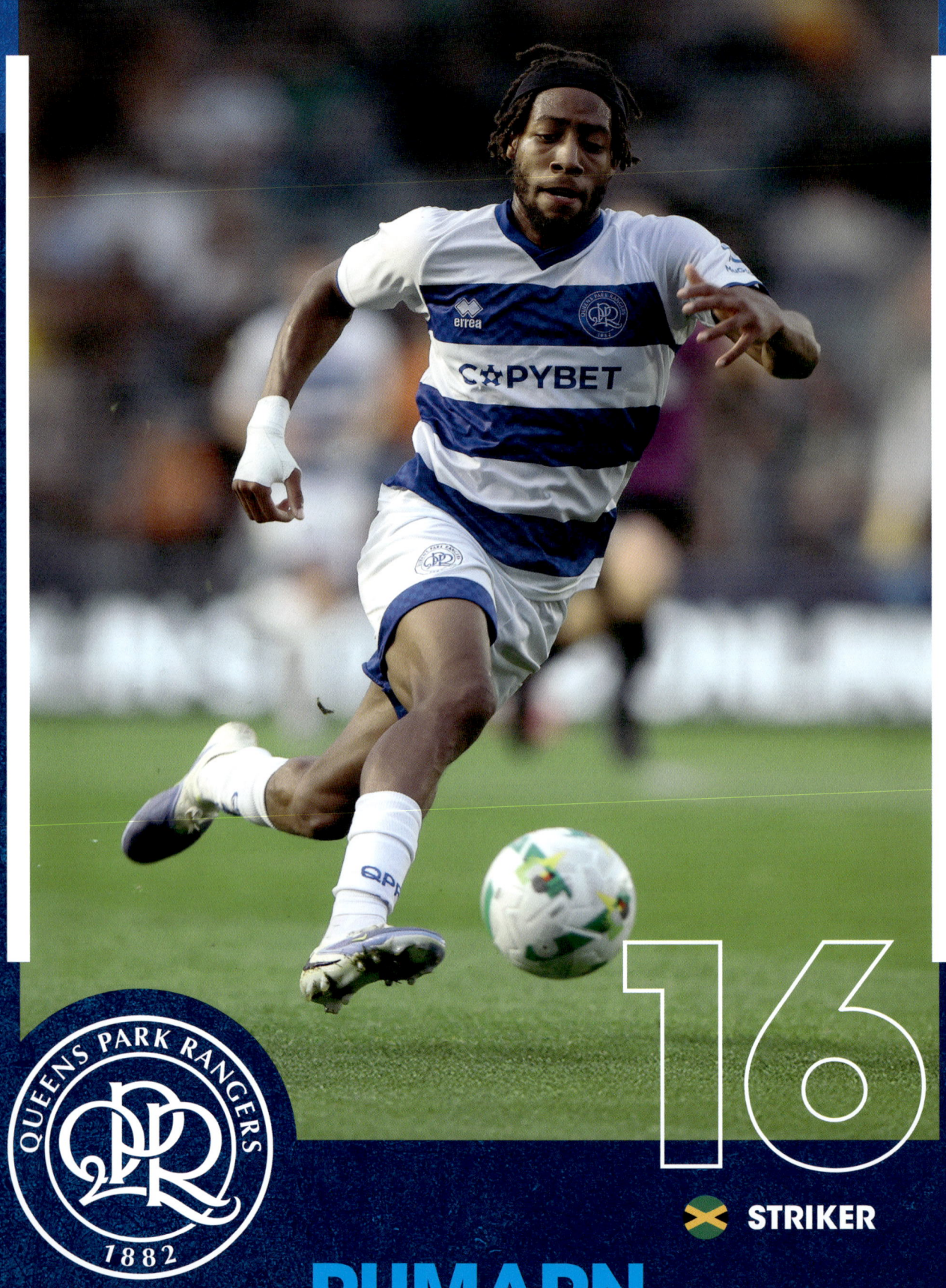

RUMARN BURRELL

16 — STRIKER

KWAME POKU

17 — MIDFIELDER

FOCUS ON

NATIONALITY: Swiss

POSITION: Striker

MARRIED: Yes, to my wife Melis

CHILDREN: Not yet

CAR: Range Rover, but I like Ferraris!

FAVOURITE TV PROGRAMME: Last Dance (Michael Jordan)

FAVOURITE PLAYER IN WORLD FOOTBALL: Zlatan Ibrahimovic

MOST PROMISING TEAM-MATE: Rayan Kolli

FAVOURITE MEAL: Zweifel chips

FAVOURITE HOLIDAY DESTINATION: Formentera

FAVOURITE PERSONALITY (I.E. COMEDIAN, ACTOR): Muhammad Ali – the greatest of all-time

FAVOURITE ACTIVITY ON DAY OFF: Time with my wife is the time of my life!

FAVOURITE MUSICIAN / BAND: Coldplay

POST-MATCH ROUTINE: MD-1 dinner – chicken with pesto pasta and half a cucumber

MICHI FREY

FAVOURITE TEAM APART FROM QPR: Bayern Munich

CHILDHOOD FOOTBALLING HERO: Zinedine Zidane

FAVOURITE SPORT OTHER THAN FOOTBALL: Table tennis

MOST DIFFICULT OPPONENT SO FAR (PLAYER): Luka Modric

MOST MEMORABLE MATCH OF YOUR CAREER: I scored five goals in one game against Standard Lüttich away!

BIGGEST DISAPPOINTMENT IN FOOTBALL SO FAR: LOSC Lille

BEST FRIEND IN FOOTBALL: Marco Bürki, now the captain of FC Thun

BIGGEST CAREER INFLUENCE: My former agent Milos Malenovic and my private physio

PERSONAL LIFE AMBITION: Play in the Premier League and for the national team of Switzerland

IF YOU WEREN'T A FOOTBALLER, WHAT WOULD YOU BE: Artist (painter)

PERSON IN WORLD YOU'D MOST LIKE TO MEET: Pablo Picasso

THE BIG QPR QUIZ

The 2024/25 season was another action-packed one for the R's. How much of it do you remember?

Take our bumper quiz to find out!

1. Which kit did QPR wear in the pre-season friendly versus Tottenham Hotspur?

2. Where do the symbols come from that appeared in both the away shirt and third shirt?

3. Which player scored in the first home match of the season; a 3-1 defeat to WBA?

4. QPR won their Carabao Cup tie versus Luton Town in a penalty shoot-out in August 2024 at MATRADE Loftus Road. What was the shoot-out scoreline?

5. Also in August 2024 the R's won their first league match of the season 2-1 away at which club?

6. In that first win who scored the two goals for QPR?

7. QPR had to wait until November 27th for their second league win of the season away at Cardiff City. Who scored for the Hoops in that 2-0 victory?

8. The first home league win of the season came at the start of December against which team?

9. Who wore the number seven shirt for the R's during season 2024/25?

10. How many shades of blue were there on the QPR home shirt from the '24/25 campaign?

11. Goalkeeper Paul Nardi was signed from which Belgian club?

12. Who is the loan player who wore the number 47 shirt?

13. Which club did loanee Ronnie Edwards join from?

14. QPR did the league double over three teams during the '24/25 season, who were they?

15. Which player bagged our 'goal of the season' and who was it scored against?

16. Which two QPR players made the joint-most first-team appearances for the R's over the course of the season?

17. Which QPR striker scored the equaliser away at Sheffield United at the start of the season only to be sold shortly afterwards?

18. Which player ended up being the leading scorer for the Hoops during '24/25?

CONTINUED ON NEXT PAGE >

19. Which player scored his first of the season at home to Norwich and went on to score four goals in total?

20. Koki Saito wore which number on his shirt?

21. Alfie Lloyd scored his first senior goal in a scrappy goalmouth scramble in the last seconds of the match away at which club?

22. Which player received the most yellow cards during the '24/25 campaign?

23. Three players received their marching orders last season, receiving red cards, who were they?

24. Which player scooped both players' player and supporters' player of the season?

25. Who was the player loaned to QPR from Newcastle United?

26. Which team was thumped 4-0 in QPR's biggest win of the season?

27. Who wore squad number 40?

28. Name the QPR signing from Chelsea who didn't make an appearance during the season owing to injury.

29. Which player scored the Hoops' last goal of the campaign away to Sunderland in a 1-0 victory?

30. How many league wins did the Super Hoops manage during the season?

YOUR FINAL SCORE /30

Answers on page 61.

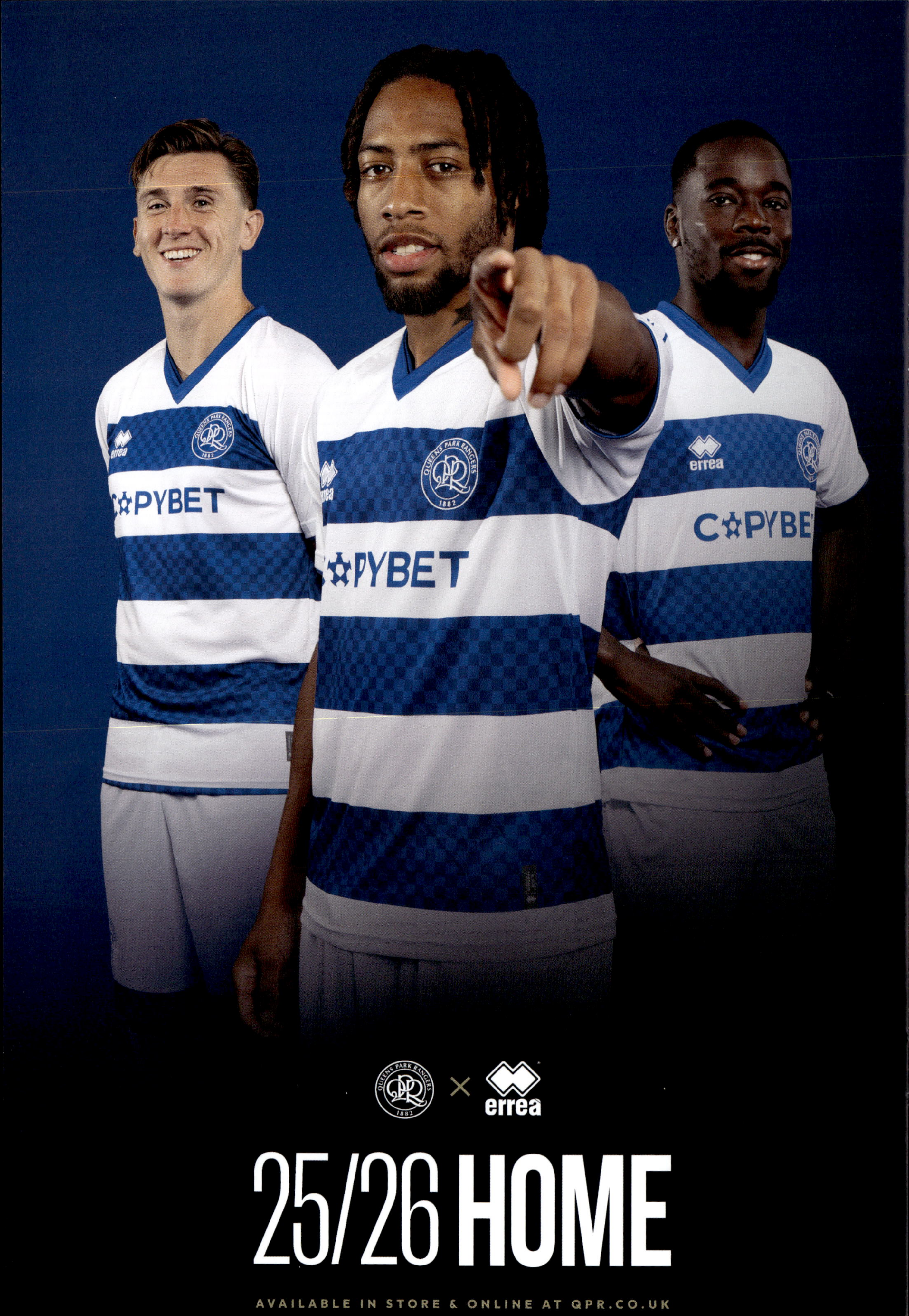
errea
25/26 HOME
AVAILABLE IN STORE & ONLINE AT QPR.CO.UK

25/26 AWAY
QUEENS PARK RANGERS

AVAILABLE IN STORE & ONLINE AT QPR.CO.UK

FOCUS ON

KIERAN MORGAN

NATIONALITY: English

POSITION: Midfielder

MARRIED: No

CHILDREN: No

CAR: Volkswagen

FAVOURITE TV PROGRAMME: Prison Break

FAVOURITE PLAYER IN WORLD FOOTBALL: Declan Rice

MOST PROMISING TEAM-MATE: Jack McDowell

FAVOURITE MEAL: Roast dinner

FAVOURITE HOLIDAY DESTINATION: Greece

FAVOURITE PERSONALITY (I.E. COMEDIAN, ACTOR): Kevin Hart

FAVOURITE ACTIVITY ON DAY OFF: Golf

FAVOURITE MUSICIAN / BAND: Coldplay

POST-MATCH ROUTINE: Have a meal and sleep

BEST FRIEND IN FOOTBALL: Matteo Salamon

FAVOURITE TEAM APART FROM QPR: Gillingham

CHILDHOOD FOOTBALLING HERO: Simeon Jackson

FAVOURITE SPORT OTHER THAN FOOTBALL: Padel

MOST DIFFICULT OPPONENT SO FAR (PLAYER): Wilfried Gnontoc

MOST MEMORABLE MATCH OF YOUR CAREER: Scoring my first goal against Coventry

BIGGEST DISAPPOINTMENT IN FOOTBALL SO FAR: Getting released from Tottenham

BIGGEST CAREER INFLUENCE: Family

PERSONAL LIFE AMBITION: Play in the Premier League

IF YOU WEREN'T A FOOTBALLER, WHAT WOULD YOU BE: A tennis player

PERSON IN WORLD YOU'D MOST LIKE TO MEET: Michael Phelps

KADER
DEMBELE

MIDFIELDER
7

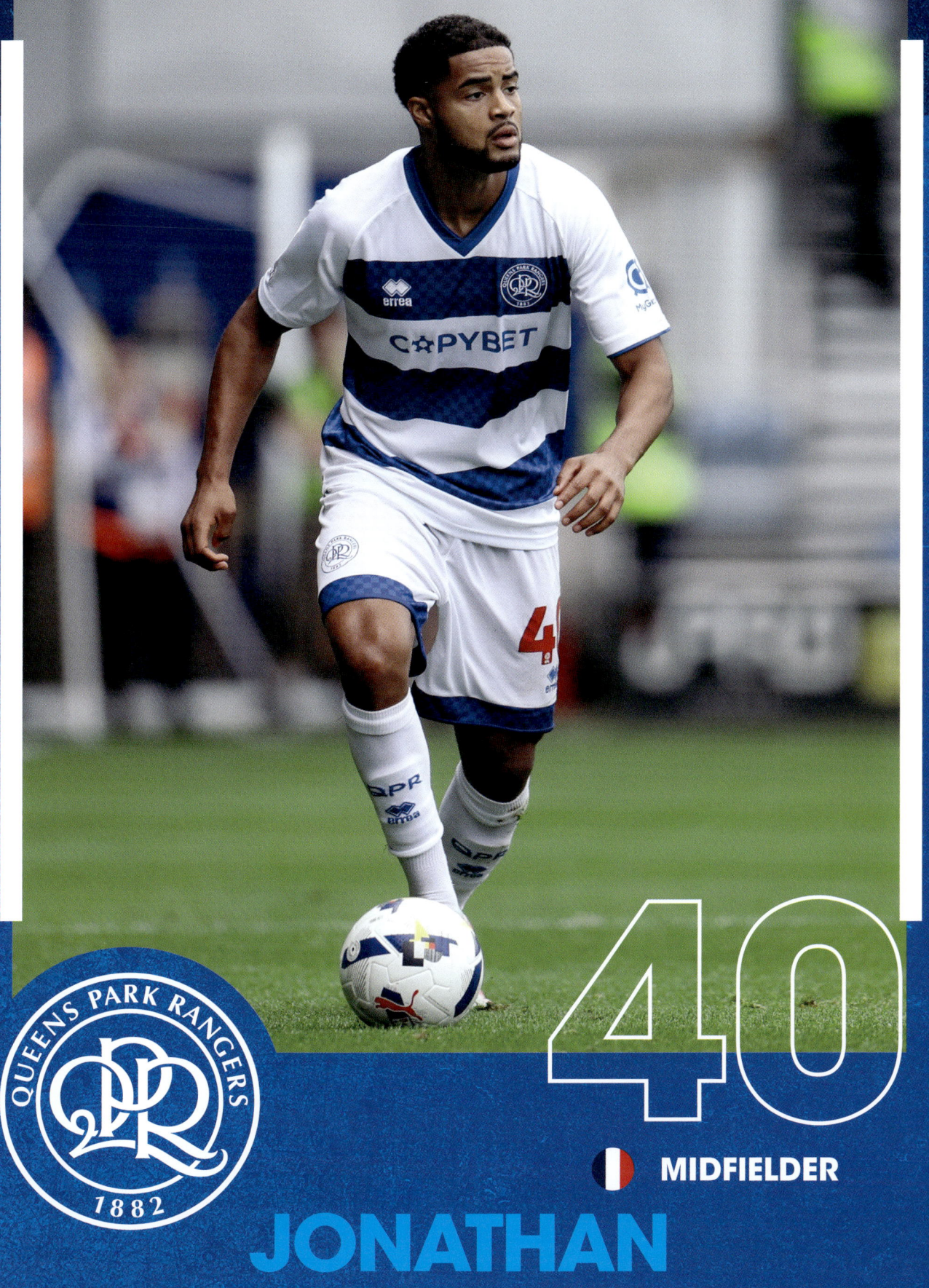

JONATHAN VARANE

40 — MIDFIELDER

ANSWERS

28 YOU ARE THE REF

1. Restart by having the penalty kick retaken.
2. The game must be restarted with a throw-in as the offence happened when the ball was not in play.
3. Restart play with an indirect free-kick.
4. A. No action, there is no offence in playing the ball twice.
5. B. If the match really can't be played for the full period you will have to abandon the match, but whenever possible the match should be played to the end.
6. B. Award an indirect free-kick for dangerous play.
7. B. Send him off as by refusing to give his number he is committing a second offence.
8. B. Award the goal... The defender's action of leaving the pitch without permission should not be allowed to gain an advantage.
9. An indirect free-kick to the opposition. The kick will have to be taken on the goal area line which runs parallel to the goal line in the nearest point to the offence.
10. Send the player off. He has still tried to strike an opponent so it's a red card.

45 GUESS THE PLAYERS

1. Field / Mbengue / Vale
2. Adamson / Dunne / Kolli
3. Dembele / Morgan / Varane

50 THE BIG QPR QUIZ

1. Gold third
2. Old Hammersmith club crest
3. Lucas Andersen
4. 4-1
5. Luton Town
6. Nicolas Madsen and Michael Frey
7. Žan Celar (2)
8. Norwich City
9. Kader Dembele
10. 3
11. Gent
12. Yang Min-Hyeok
13. Southampton
14. Luton Town, Oxford United and Preston North End
15. Paul Smyth at Bristol City
16. Paul Nardi and Jimmy Dunne
17. Lyndon Dykes
18. Michael Frey (8)
19. Rayan Kolli
20. 14
21. Sheffield Wednesday
22. Jimmy Dunne (9)
23. Jonathan Varane, Jack Colback & Koki Saito
24. Jimmy Dunne
25. Harrison Ashby
26. Derby County
27. Jonathan Varane
28. Harvey Vale
29. Nicolas Madsen
30. 13

44 WORDSEARCH

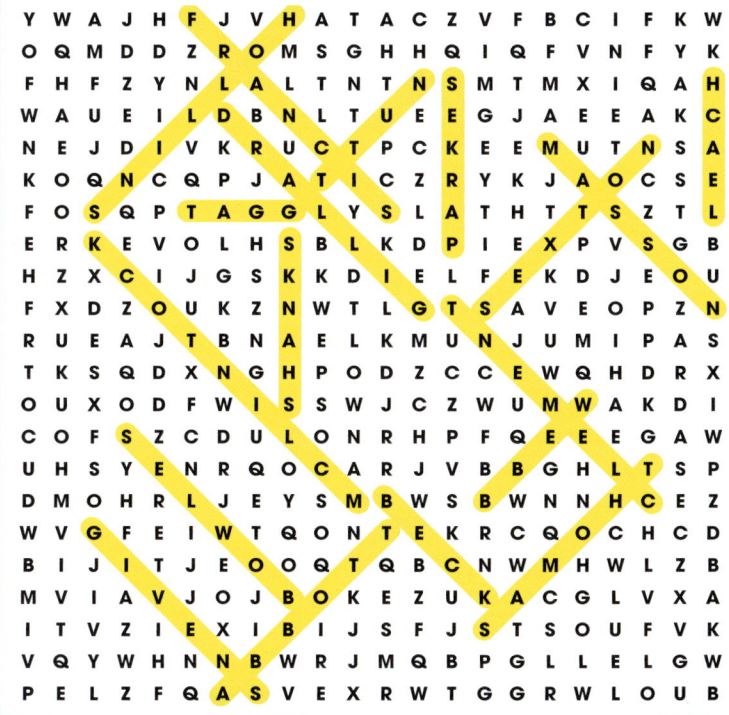

FIXTURES

QPR'S 2025/26 SKY BET CHAMPIONSHIP SCHEDULE

DATE	OPPONENTS		SCORE
SAT 9 AUG	PRESTON NORTH END	H	
SAT 16 AUG	WATFORD	A	
SAT 23 AUG	COVENTRY	A	
SAT 30 AUG	CHARLTON ATHLETIC	H	
SAT 13 SEPT	WREXHAM	A	
SAT 20 SEPT	STOKE CITY	H	
SAT 27 SEPT	SHEFFIELD WED	A	
WED 1 OCT	OXFORD UNITED	H	
SAT 4 OCT	BRISTOL CITY	A	
SAT 18 OCT	MILLWALL	H	
WED 22 OCT	SWANSEA CITY	A	
SAT 25 OCT	DERBY COUNTY	A	
SAT 1 NOV	IPSWICH TOWN	H	
WED 5 NOV	SOUTHAMPTON	H	
SAT 8 NOV	SHEFFIELD UNITED	A	
SAT 22 NOV	HULL CITY	H	
WED 26 NOV	BLACKBURN ROVERS	A	
SAT 29 NOV	NORWICH CITY	A	
SAT 6 DEC	WEST BROM	H	
TUE 9 DEC	BIRMINGHAM CITY	H	
SAT 13 DEC	MIDDLESBROUGH	A	
SAT 20 DEC	LEICESTER CITY	H	
FRI 26 DEC	PORTSMOUTH	A	
MON 29 DEC	WEST BROM	A	
THU 1 JAN	NORWICH CITY	H	
SUN 4 JAN	SHEFFIELD WED	H	
SAT 17 JAN	STOKE CITY	A	
TUE 20 JAN	OXFORD UNITED	A	
SAT 24 JAN	WREXHAM	H	
SAT 31 JAN	COVENTRY CITY	H	
SAT 7 FEB	CHARLTON ATHLETIC	A	
SAT 14 FEB	BLACKBURN ROVERS	H	
SAT 21 FEB	HULL CITY	A	
TUE 24 FEB	SOUTHAMPTON	A	
SAT 28 FEB	SHEFFIELD UNITED	H	
SAT 7 MAR	MIDDLESBROUGH	H	
TUE 10 MAR	BIRMINGHAM CITY	A	
SAT 14 MAR	LEICESTER CITY	A	
SAT 21 MAR	PORTSMOUTH	H	
FRI 3 APR	WATFORD	H	
MON 6 APR	PRESTON NORTH END	A	
SAT 11 APR	BRISTOL CITY	H	
SAT 18 APR	MILLWALL	A	
TUE 21 APR	SWANSEA CITY	H	
SAT 25 APR	DERBY COUNTY	H	
SAT 2 MAY	IPSWICH TOWN	A	